To the Proprietors of *Punch* and *Baily's Magazine*, and to the Editors of *The Field*, *Country Life*, *Westminster Gazette*, *Scottish Field*, *British Australasian*, and *Scotsman*, the Author gratefully acknowledges permission to reproduce verses first published in their columns

GALLOPING SHOES

HARK TO THE MUSICAL SPICK OF THE HOOFS
BY THE ROAD WHERE THE DITCHES ARE READY TO RUN!

VERSES

BY

WILL H. OGILVIE

ILLUSTRATIONS BY

LIONEL EDWARDS

LONDON

CONSTABLE AND COMPANY LTD

Printed in Great Britain by T and A Constab
at the University Press, Edinburgh

TO YOU!

Here's to you, Stocking and Star and Blaze!
  You brought me all that the best could bring—
Health and Mirth and the Merriest Days
In the Open Fields and the Woodland Ways—
  And what can I do in return, but sing
A song or two in your praise!

W H. O.

CONTENTS

THE BLAST OF THE HORN

THE CALL OF THE BUGLE

THE CLINK OF THE BIT

LIST OF ILLUSTRATIONS

THE BLAST OF THE HORN

HYMN TO DIANA

DIAN ! Hear us when we pray.
   Send us foxes fleet and strong,
Grass to speed them on their way,
   Hounds to hustle them along !
   Hunters that can do no wrong,
Fences stout and ditches deep,
   That our place among the throng
May be worth our while to keep !

By the blood of which we came,
   Make us sportsmen unafraid ;
Grant us that we play the game
   Straightly as it should be played,
   Giving place and giving aid
As a comrade may require,
   Bringing pride but to be laid
On thy glowing altar-fire.

Dian ! Goddess of the Chase,

HYMN TO DIANA

Grant that we may take our place
   With the boldest of the bold ,
   But if Chance her best withhold
And a fence our fate supply,
   Let us, low amid the mould,
Cheer the chase as it goes by !

THE GAME OF OUR HEARTS

THIS is the game of our hearts !
   Foot to the stirrup ! Away !
Care with the night departs,
   Joy comes in with the day.
A good horse tossing his rings,
   A light rime decking the thorn :
And the heart of the horseman sings
   For love of a hunting morn.

This is the game of our hearts !
   Mottled flanks in the fern ;
Rate where a rabbit starts,
   Cheer to a waving stern ;
Call that we rush to obey
   From a Whip at his post outside :
Gone away ! Gone aw-a-a-ay !
   And we sit down to ride.

This is the game of our hearts !
   Crash and rattle of rail ;
Lean hounds driving like darts

Tried Age taking the lead,
  Rash Youth coated with clay ;
Glory and glamour of speed,
  And a right fox away.

This is the game of our hearts,
  Whatever luck may ensue—
This, where a Master of Arts
  May fail and a dunce get throug
This, where the confident thrust ;
  This, where the cowardly crane ;
This, where there 's nothing to trus
  But fate and the feel of the rein.

This is the game of our hearts !
  Squire and lawyer and lord,
Men of the farms and the marts,
  Men of the pen and the sword ;
Comrades we jog to the meet,
  Rivals we ride the line,
And the sound of the hoofs is sweet
  And the taste of the wind is wine

THE OPENING RUN

THE rain-sodden grass in the ditches is dying,
  The berries are red to the crest of the thorn ;
Coronet-deep where the beech leaves are lying
  The hunters stand tense to the twang of the horn ,
Where rides are re-filled with the green of the mosses,
  All foam-flecked and fretful their long line is strung,
You can see the white gleam as a starred forehead
    tosses,
  You can hear the low chink as a bit-bar is flung.

The world 's full of music. Hounds rustle the rover
  Through brushwood and fern to a glad ' Gone
    away ! '
With a ' Come along, Pilot ! '—one spur-touch and
    over—
  The huntsman is clear on his galloping grey ;
Before him the pack 's running straight on the
    stubble—
  ' *Toot-toot-too-too-too-oot !* '—' *Tow-row-ow-ow-ow !* '
The leaders are clambering up through the double

The front rank, hands down, have the big fence's
    measure ;
  The faint hearts are craning to left and to right ;
The Master goes through with a crash on The
    Treasure,
  The grey takes the lot like a gull in his flight.
There 's a brown crumpled up, lying still as a dead
    one ;
  There 's a roan mare refusing, as stubborn as sin,
While the breaker flogs up on a green underbred one
  And smashes the far-away rail with a grin

The chase carries on over hilltop and hollow,
  The life of Old England, the pluck and the fun ;
And who would ask more than a stiff line to follow
  With hounds running hard in the Opening Run ?

WITH A 'COME ALONG, PILOT!'—ONE SPUR TOUCH AND OVER—
THE HUNTSMAN IS CLEAR ON HIS GALLOPING GREY;

('THE OPENING RUN.')

THE FIRST FLIGHT

WHILE there 's one on his feet with a tale to repeat
    And another is sampling a drink,
The eager First Flight have a girth to draw tight
    Or a chain to let out by a link ;
While the boisterous laugh in that circle of chaff
    The opening music has drowned,
You will hear the First Flight as they whisper ' That 's
      right ! '
    To the note of a favourite hound.

When a holloa makes sure that his start is secure
    And dispels every doubt of a run,
When the crowd gallops straight to the obvious
      gate
    With the latch that is never undone,
You will see the First Flight cram a topper on
      tight,
    Catch a willing old nag by the head,
And clapping on sail at the blackthorn or rail,

They thunder away over stubble and clay,
   Over roots or the level o' lea,
The gallant First Flight that are soon out of sight
   While the slow ones are sadly at sea.
The crash of a rail in the cream of the vale
   Is to them but a matter of mirth,
And the avalanche fall of a hoof-rattled wall
   But the merriest music on earth.

There are gaps, there are gates for the coward who
      waits,
   There are roads for the fellow who fears ;
To left nor to right go the gallant First Flight
   Save to veer with the chase as it veers
No field has a fence so dark-looming and dense
   Or a rail so unyielding and stout
But if once the First Flight have got in it all right
   You may trust them to find a way out.

Now the men who ride first may be frequently cursed
   As they press on the faltering pack,
But we 're all of us loth to pull up for an oath
   When it comes from a field or two back ;
And the Master may blame and the jealous declaim,
   But the weakest must go to the wall,
And it 's plain the First Flight have the premier right
   If the hounds may be hustled at all.

Come drink with me, then, to the big-hearted men
  Who have pluck to sit down and go straight !
Whether farmer or squire may they keep out of wire
  And be spared a lift home on a gate !
Fill your glasses to-night to the gallant First Flight,
  Let us wish them the luck of the line
And to-morrow's recall to the best game of all,
  And the wind that is better than wine !

THE VETERAN

He asks no favour from the Field, no forward place
    demands,
Save what he claims by fearless heart and light and
    dainty hands ;
No man need make a way for him at ditch or gap or
    gate,
He rides on level terms with all, if not at equal weight.

His eyes are somewhat dimmer than they were in
    days of yore,
A blind fence now might trap him where it never
    trapped before ;
But when the rails stand clean and high, the walls
    stand big and bare,
There 's no man rides so boldly as there 's no man
    rides so fair.

There is no other in the Field so truly loved as he ;
We better like to see him out than any younger three ;
And yet one horseman day by day rides jealous at
    his rein—
Old Time that smarts beneath the whip of fifty years'
    disdain.

He crowds him at his fences, for he envies his renown ,
Some day he 'll cross him at a leap and bring a good
    man down,
And Time will take a long revenge for years of laugh-
    ing scorn,
And fold the faded scarlet that was ne'er more nobly
    worn.

Here 's luck ! Oh ! good, grey sportsman ! May
    Time be long defied
By careful seat and cunning hand and health and
    heart to ride,
And when that direful day be come that surely shall
    befall,
We 'll know you still unbeaten, save by Time that
    beats us all !

THE PERFECT HAT

THE Bowler and the Wide-awake,
  The Topper and the Straw,
The Homburg and the Helmet
  May be hats without a flaw ;
The Bonnet of the Highlanders,
  The Busby of the Greys
Are hats we shall remember
  To the end of all our days ;
The Jockey-cap of sunlit silk,
  The Bishop's Shovel-black
Can honour a cathedral town
  Or grace a racing track.
But the neatest, sweetest headgear,
  Be it e'er so crushed or crude,
Is the Hat upon the Skyline
  When a forward fox is viewed.

It may be grimy, green with age,
  Or stained with tar or muck,
Yet never flew so fair a flag
  From tower or mizzen-truck

And when we see it waving there
　　Against the wintry sky
We know the leading hounds are right,
　　And soon a fox shall die.
That holloa on the windy height
　　That sounds above the gale
Will send them racing o'er the ridge,
　　And chiming down the vale.
Salute it, then—The Perfect Hat,
　　However grimed and green—
The Hat upon the Skyline
　　When our sinking fox is seen !

TOM MOODY

DEATH had beckoned with grisly hand
To the finest Whip in hunting-land.

'My time is short,' Tom Moody said,
' Master, when I am done and dead,

Lay me at Barrow beneath the yew
In the dear old shire we have hunted through.

Let six earth-stoppers carry me there
With slow step and heads bare.

Bring the old horse that I used to ride,
With my whip and boots to his saddle tied.

Fasten the brush in his forehead-band
Of the last dog-fox we brought to hand.

And let a couple of old hounds come,
Fitting mourners to follow me home.

Then, when you 've laid me safe down there,
Give three view-holloas will shake the air,

And you 'll know, if I do not lift my head,
There is no mistake—Tom Moody 's dead !'

AND WHEN WE SEE IT WAVING THERE,
AGAINST THE WINTRY SKY,
WE KNOW THE LEADING HOUNDS ARE RIGHT,
AND SOON A FOX SHALL DIE.

THE MOON-RAKER

Not the lord of copse or covert
   Lying lazy in the sun,
But the late returning lover
   Is the fox we fain would run,
Stealing home across the meadows
   In the glare and dust of noon
Like an exile of the shadows
   Filled with memories of the moon.

As the cigarettes are lighted,
   While the rein is on the wrist,
For a moment he is sighted
   Ere he melts away like mist ;
And our bridles we recover,
   And we fling our weeds away,
For we know that moonlight lover
   Means to make the pace to-day.

He is scarce a field before us
   When a lifted cap for sign
Sets a sixteen-couple chorus
   Chiming loudly on his line.

We shall learn before it 's over
  Just how far a fox can roam,
And the pace of a night-rover
  When his mask is set for home.

With that one endeavour burning
  He will lead us, straight of neck ;
There 'll be neither twist nor turning,
  There 'll be neither pause nor check ,
We shall learn by each disaster,
  Rotten bank and breaking bar,
There is nothing travels faster
  Than a homing Lochinvar.

All we ask for is a rover
  That the waking Spring beguiles
To go forth and meet a lover
  Over many moonlit miles.
May there sound the sudden holloa
  That discovers him next day,
And may I be there to follow
  When that rover leads the way !

HOUNDS IN LONDON

WHAT are you doing here, you cluster of mottled
    beauty,
  Far from the fields you love and the copses scented
    sweet,
Treading the stones of London at the call of some
    strange new duty,
  You that should run with the beech-leaves rustling
    over your feet ?

You that are free of the woodlands, what can you find
    but scorning
  For the long unplanted pavements and the tall
    unbranching roofs ?
You that have heard the south wind sing loud on a
    hunting morning,
  When lanes were flashing with scarlet and fields
    were drumming with hoofs ?
      *   *   *   *   *   *
If they find you a fox in Mayfair, will you show them
    a right pack running,
  With scorn of a Hyde Park holloa or a hat held up

If he leads you into the Gardens where the trees
      stand tall and quiet,
  Will you carry it on by the water as only a good
      pack can ?
Will you tarry not for the children's call nor turn
      aside to riot
  Where sit by their sandless burrows the rabbits of
      Peter Pan ?

If you pass the towering Needle when the shadows
      of dusk are falling,
  And gold on the magic water are the lights of the
      little piers,
Will your heads go up for a moment when you hear
      old Egypt calling,
  Thrilling a distant ' For'ard on ! ' out of the dusk
      of years ?

Will you throw your tongues of silver till the spires
      on the churches quiver ?
  Will you glitter beneath the arches till the road is
      a cloud of white ?

Will you fling from the bank and follow if he crosses
    London River,
To show that your fox is forward and show that
    your hearts are right ?

   *   *   *   *   *   *

Somewhere are friends that need you ; somewhere
    are wet woods waiting ;
Somewhere are clean green pastures with a clean
    cool wind above,—
'Tis time to be footing the dance again to a tune of
    your own creating,
Leading the men that love you over the vale you
    love !

THE THAW

HARK to the avalanche snow from the roofs
   O'er eaves where the icicles melt in the sun !
Hark to the musical suck of the hoofs
   By the road where the ditches are ready to run !
On the slope of the hill is a patchwork of green
   And the fallows are spotted with spaces of brown,
While woodlands and copses and hedges between
      Have lost the white burden that weighted them
         down.

The silence that came with the fall of the frost
   Has broken in patter and tinkle and drip,
And murmur of wind where the pinetops are tossed
   To the outermost, furthermost feathery tip
The pigeons are back on the ridge of the roofs
   And the sparrows a-twitter once more in the sun,
But dearer than all is the suck of the hoofs
   That tells to the sportsman the thaw has begun.

You may sing of the diamond gems on the thorn
 And the hedges all hung with a silvery sheen,
But nothing does winter so fitly adorn
 As the first flashing jewels of emerald green !
Good-bye to King Frost and his murderous grip,
 Let the snow and her silvery servants withdraw !
Let us back to the horn and the hound and the whip ;
 Be the ploughs e'er so heavy, good luck to the
  thaw !

THE RAIDERS

WHERE the gorse standeth deep
  On the slopes of the hill,
Where the westerlies sweep
  O'er the wold at their will,
In a glade of old grass
  That the winter has seared
And the winds as they pass
  Have not noticed or neared,
Restless-eyed, ready-eared
  Every danger to shun,
The little red foxes lie out in the sun.

When the stars are aglow
  And the cloud is alight
With the moonflowers that grow
  From the leaves of the night,
In the shadow and hush
  Of the undergrowth dank
There 's a stir in the brush,
  And a step on the bank,
And the gleam of a flank
  Where the thorn leaves are strewn—
And the little red foxes steal forth by the moon.

Ere the stars are grown dim,
   Ere the moon 's out of sight,
Ere the dawn sings her hymn
   To the rose of the light,
Leaping over the heath,
   Creeping low in the fern,
With their spoil in their teeth
   The red rovers return ;
But ere long they shall learn
   Retribution unbars
Swift wrath on the raiders that steal by the stars

YOUNG ENGLAND

FOAM upon their snaffle-bars, forelocks flying free,
    Busy little Shetlands battle up the ride ;
Cream below the crupper-straps, mud above the knee :
    Vieing with the hunters that pass them in a
        stride.

Rosy-cheeked and eager, firm as little rocks,
    Down upon their saddles, keen and full of fire,
Ride the youth of England. *One has seen the fox !*
    One has had a tumble, tripping over wire !

Every passing hoof-beat sends them to the whip ;
    Every thrilling horn-blast drives an anxious
        heel ,
Every ' Come on, Billy boy ! ' starts a quivering
        lip ;
    What can man do more than give 'em whip and
        steel !

Now they 're in the open, reaching at the bit ;
    Every furry neck is stretched racing on the grass ,
' Shake 'em up ' is now the word, old or fat or fit—
    While there is a pony in front of them to pass.
26

All the rush and rapture was not fashioned for the few
    Sweeping at the big brook splendid in their
    speed ;
Youth is there behind you just as keen as you,
    Fretting to be forward, longing for the lead

Give them room for galloping ; youth will find its
    year,
    Time will cap them forward and cheer them to
    a place ;
Dappled hounds will run for them, horses jump like
    deer
    These will keep in England the glory of the
    Chase.

THE HILL MEN

Mark you that group as it stands by the stell !—
    Here is no ponderous pride,
Here is no swagger, no place for the swell,
    But a handful of fellows who 'll ride
A fox to his death over upland and fell
    Where a hundred good foxes have died.

Here is the Master of Hounds—take note !—
    On a rough horse run on the farm ;
And here is the Whip in a rusty coat
    With a terrier under his arm,
And a holloa hid in his rough red throat
    To work hill-foxes harm.

And here is the pack, from their benches torn
    Long ever the cocks had crowed,
To follow the hint of the Master's horn
    Through the mist of the moorland road ;
Half of them lame, with pads red-worn
    On the screes where the shingle showed.

And here 's the covert , no woodland wide
 But a bunch of stunted whin—
A place where a mouse could hardly hide
 Or a spider find room to spin.
The Master, up in his stirrups to ride,
 Is cheering them ' Leu, boys, in ! '

Scarce have they quested a quarter through
 With their sterns all waving gay,
When the hills are rent with a hullabaloo
 And the fellow they want is away—
A great hill-fox running right in view
 With his mask to the Merlin Brae.

Up by the glidders he glides and goes
 To his stronghold under the scar,
But a shepherd was there ere the sun-god rose
 And his door shows bolt and bar,
So he turns his head to the south ; he knows
 It is time to go fast and far.

Over the top come the lean white hounds
 Screaming to scent and view ;
The hills are waked to their furthest bounds
 As they clamour and drive him through,
And the joy of the far-flung challenge sounds
 Till it shivers against the blue.

' Faith, and it is ! '   Bob, riding blind,
    Comes slithering over the screes,
His pony now on its fat behind
    And now on its battered knees—
' He had legs as long as a foal, I mind,
    And a trunk as big as a tree's.'

Says Bill · ' There 's a stranger stuck in the bog
    With nowt but his head in sight,
And there he may lie like a drain-fast hogg
    Till the hounds come back at night
Look ye, man Dave, at yon old white dog
    Going over the top—yon 's right ! '
      *   *   *   *   *   *
A holloa breaks from the hills ahead
    And an answering ' For'ard on ! '
There 's a clatter down in the burn's rough bed ;
    Then the mist drops weird and wan ;
The rubble rings to a clinking tread
    Far off—and the hunt is gone.

MOTHER HUBBARD

THE south wind was whispering low in the firs,
   A pale sun was gilding the curve of the hill
When we turned on to grass with a touch of the spurs
   And caught up the crowd below Dittany Mill.
She greeted the scarlet, as always her way,
   With a plunge and a kick disconcertingly high,
And I knew if Fate gave us a galloping day
   We should set them the pace, Mother Hubbard
      and I.

Hounds were scarce through the ditch into Dittany
      Gorse
   When they found him, and out over banking and rail
Came the huntsman full tilt on his thoroughbred
      horse,
   And blew them away down the best of the vale.
A hundred keen horsemen rode hard in his wake
   Over sound-going grass where the low meadows lie ;
There were hedges to crash through and binders to
      break,

The brook in the bottom took more than its share—
   How many were down in it nobody knows !—
She reefed and she raced at it, good little mare ;
   And I held her—then gave her the rein as she rose.
She sailed into space like a bird in its flight ;
   There was nothing in front but a glint of the sky.
Then she landed as softly as sea-gulls alight.—
   We had pounded the field, Mother Hubbard and I.

Behind us, we knew, was the cream of the Hunt,
   Collecting its hat and comparing its ills,
While the best pack in England was screaming in front
   On the line of a hill-fox away to his hills.
Full speed up the broad river-meadows we flew ,
   The fence at the top was both solid and high,
But we had it exactly where hounds had gone through,
   And we had it alone, Mother Hubbard and I.

The straps of her breastplate were lathered in white
   As we slanted the slope, and her flanks were a-foam,
For a horseman must ride like a wind of the night
   When the mask of a hill-fox is set for his home ;
But she cocked a brown ear to the clamorous call
   That rose with the breeze as it racketed by,
And like mist on the moor we slid over the wall
   And went galloping on, Mother Hubbard and I.
     *   *   *   *   *   *

WE HAD KILLED HIM ALONE UNDER BEVERLY'S BOUNDS,
AND HAD TORN HIM TO PIECES IN SIGHT OF HIS EARTH.
MOTHER HUBBARD.

It was dusk when the huntsman took over his hounds
  As we turned down the lane with the brush at our
     girth ;
We had killed him alone under Beverly's Bounds
  And had torn him to pieces in sight of his earth.
The wind rose. Around us the beech-leaves were
     whirled
  And purple the clouds scurried over the sky,
But proud and contented—at peace with the world—
  We splashed through the pools, Mother Hubbard
     and I.

HACKING HOME

WHEN your homing carloads swing
   Past us down the crisping lanes,
And your dazzling headlights fling
   Snow-white roses on our reins,
Would we choose your sheltered flight,
   Would we take your cushioned ease
For the wide and scented night
   And the horse between our knees ?

Breezes that your wheels o'erleap
   Whisper round us as we ride ;
Ours the star-bedusted deep
   That your misted windows hide ;
And while speed may waft you soon
   To your halls of warmth and light,
Is not ours the magic moon
   Spilling silver from the night ?

A SINGLE HOUND

When the opal lights in the West had died
  And night was wrapping the red ferns round,
As I came home by the woodland side
  I heard the cry of a single hound

The huntsman had gathered his pack and gone ;
  The last late hoof had echoed away ;
The horn was twanging a long way on
  For the only hound that was still astray.

While, heedless of all but the work in hand,
  Up through the brake where the brambles twine,
Crying his joy to a drowsy land
  Javelin drove on a burning line.

The air was sharp with a touch of frost,
  The moon came up like a wheel of gold ;
The wall at the end of the woods he crossed
  And flung away on the open wold.

And long as I listened beside the stile
  The larches echoed that eerie sound .
Steady and tireless, mile on mile,

THE CALL OF THE BUGLE

TOP-O'-THE-MORNING

(1914)

TOP-O'-THE MORNING'S shoes are off ;
    He runs in the orchard, rough, all day,
Chasing the hens for a turn at the trough,
    Fighting the cows for a place at the hay ;
With a coat where the Wiltshire mud has dried,
    With brambles twined in his mane and tail—
Top-o'-the-Morning, pearl and pride
    Of the foremost flight of the White Horse Vale !

The master he carried is Somewhere in France
    Leading a cavalry troop to-day,
Ready if Fortune but give him the chance,
    Ready as ever to show them the way.
Riding as straight to his new desire
    As ever he rode to the line of old,
Facing his fences of blood and fire
    With a brow of flint and a heart of gold.

Do the hoofs of his horses wake a dream
    Of a trampling crowd at the covert-side,
Of a lead on the grass and a glinting stream
    And Top-o'-the-Morning shortening stride ?

Does the triumph leap to his shining eyes
  As the wind of the vale on his cheek blows cold,
And the buffeting big brown shoulders rise
  To his light heel's touch and his light hand's hold ?

When the swords are sheathed and the strife is done
  And the cry of hounds is a call to men,
When the straight-necked Wiltshire foxes run
  And the first flight crosses the grass again,
May Top-o'-the-Morning, sleek of hide,
  Shod, and tidy of mane and tail,
Light, and fit for a man to ride,
  Lead them once more in the White Horse Vale !

A HUNTSMAN GREY
WHO BLEW THEM AWAY
WITH THE NOTE OF A TRUE HOUND-LOVER.

('THE FIRST WHIP.')

THE FIRST WHIP

(1915)

As I wandered home
By Hedworth Combe
I heard a lone horse whinny,
And saw on the hill
Stand statue-still
At the top of the old oak spinney
A rough-haired hack
With a girl on his back—
And ' *Hounds !* ' I said—' *for a guinea !* '

The wind blew chill
Over Larchley Hill,
And it couldn't have blown much colder ;
Her nose was blue,
And her pigtails two
Hung damply over her shoulder ;
She might have been ten,
Or—guessing again—

To a tight pink lip
She pressed her whip
By way of imposing quiet ;
I bowed my head
To the word unsaid,
Accepting the lady's fiat,
And noted the while
Her Belvoir style
As she rated a hound for riot.

A lean form leapt
O'er the fence and crept
Through the ditch with his thief's heart quaking,
But the face of the maid
No hint betrayed
That she noticed the brambles shaking,
Till she saw him clear
Of her one wild fear—
The chance of his backward breaking.

Then dainty and neat
She rose in her seat
That the better her eyes might follow
Where a shadow of brown
Over Larchley Down
Launched out like a driving swallow ;

And she quickened his speed
Through bracken and weed
With a regular Pytchley holloa !

Raging they came
Like a torrent of flame—
There were nineteen couple and over,
And a huntsman grey
Who blew them away
With the note of a true hound-lover,
While his Whip sat back
On her rough old hack
And called to the last in covert.

Then cramming down flat
Her quaint little hat,
And shaking the old horse together,
She was off like a bird,
And the last that I heard
Was a ' For'ard ! ' that died in the heather
As she took up her place
At the tail of the chase
Like a ten-season lord of the leather.

THE GREY COMPANY

(1920)

THEIR white and their scarlet are folded away,
   The hoofs of their horses are dumb on the hill ;
In vain do we look for our comrades to-day,
   Yet we know that in spirit they ride with us still.

Not the faintest low whimper that sounds in the thorn
   But those keen ones will hear as they heard it of old ;
Not a far-away holloa or blast of the horn
   But be loud to the men who lie under the mould.

Can they sleep, can they sleep when the wind hurries
      by
   Through the woodlands of France with a rustle of
      leaves ?
In the dark and the silence content can they lie
   When the stubbles of Flanders are shorn of their
      sheaves ?

Not the long leagues between, not the seas that divide,
   Will prevent them from hearing the thunder of
      horse,

The ' Tally-ho back ! ' of a Whip in the ride,
  Or the glad ' Gone away ! ' from the end of the
    gorse.

As we cram our hats for the cream of the vale,
  By the ghosts of old comrades the pace will be set,
And the brave ones who broke for us rasper and rail
  Will be riding the grassland in front of us yet.

THE CRUTCH

(1920)

CRIPPLED, he stands beside the gate
   In the long moorland wall,
Kept out of all the fun by fate
   Yet loving it withal ;
And when the hounds with nearing cry
   Bid vain regret be gone,
He holds his crutch against the sky
   To show their fox is on.

*   *   *   *   *   *

For us he suffered in the fight,
   For us he walks in pain,
A rider in the foremost flight
   Who will not ride again ,
And we who know him best may read
   In those brave glistening eyes
The breadth of courage in our breed,
   The depth of sacrifice.

TO ONE OF OUR WOUNDED

(Reading ' Handley Cross ')

(1916)

OLD man, by your broad contented grin
   And the gleam in your quiet eyes,
You are back with *Jorrocks* and *Binjimin*
   In the land where the good fun lies ;
You are riding where rifles reach you not
   On a line both safe and sure
From the meet at the ' Cat and Custard Pot '
   To the kill on Wandermoor.

In vain do the cannon of memory call
   From the Flanders fields forlorn,
When you hear by the stacks of Barley Hall
   The twang of the ' 'ard un's ' horn ,
And little you reck of a broken thigh
   And a bandaged arm to boot,
When the old comedian canters by

For, back to you comes each sound and sight
   At a touch of the magic pen,
Till you take your place in the old first flight,
   With a lead on the grass again,
And *Surtees*, the sage with the jester's art,
   Would be proud had he lived to know
He had brightened an hour for your gallant heart
   With the ring of his ' Tally-ho ! '

THE WALER

(1916)

THERE goes a bucker, wherever they bred him,
  By the lift of his loin and the white in his
    eye ;
Wide were the paddocks, I 'll wager, that fed
    him ,
  Red were the ridges that ran to the sky !
See how those sensitive ears of his quiver !
  See how, high-headed, the crowd he disdains,
Full of the pride of the Warrego River,
  Full of the scorn of the Irrara plains !

Bit of a rogue and a renegade is he ?
  Bad to get on to and hang to and hold ?
Bent like a bow does he buck till you 're dizzy ?—
  Thus they behave where his lordship was
    foaled.
Send for that chap in the tilted sombrero,
  Cleaning a chestnut and chewing a string ;
No one, it may be, looks less of a hero,

The day will arrive when the war-front is wider,
  And swifter the squadrons will gallop and form ;
Then give him his lean-visaged, light-handed rider
  And launch him away on the leagues of the storm ;
Give him his head to the stars growing paler
  That mark where the Dawn is a symbol and sign,
And first of them all before night shall the Waler
  With foam on his muzzle drink deep of the Rhine.

THE REMOUNT TRAIN

(1915)

EVERY head across the bar,
Every blaze and snip and star,
Every nervous twitching ear,
Every soft eye filled with fear,
Seeks a friend and seems to say :
' Whither now, and where away ? '
Seeks a friend and seems to ask
' Where the goal and what the task ? '

Wave the green flag ! Let them go !—
Only horses ? Yes, I know ;
But my heart goes down the line
With them, and their grief is mine !—
There goes honour, there goes faith,
Down the way of dule and death,
Hidden in the cloud that clings
To the battle-wrath of kings !

There goes timid childlike trust
To the burden and the dust !
Highborn courage, princely grace
To the peril it must face !

Wave the flag, and let them go !—
Hats off to that wistful row
Of lean heads of brown and bay,
Black and chestnut, roan and grey !
Here 's good luck in lands afar—
Snow-white streak, and blaze, and star !
May you find in those far lands
Kindly hearts and horsemen's hands !

THE OFFSIDE LEADER

(1918)

This is the wish, as he told it to me,
Of Driver MacPherson of Battery B.

I WANT no praise, nor ribbons to wear ;
I 've done my bit, and I 've had my share
Of filth and fighting and blood and tears
And doubt and death in the last four years.
My team and I were among the first
Contemptible few when the war-clouds burst
We sweated our gun through the dust and heat,
We hauled her back in the Big Retreat,
With weary horses and short of shell,
Turning our backs on them.   That was Hell.

That was at Mons , but we came back there,
With shine on the horses and shells to spare '
And much I 've suffered and much I 've seen
From Mons to Mons on the miles between,
But I want no praise, nor ribbons to wear—
All I ask for my fighting share
Is this   that England will give to me
My offside leader in Battery B.

She was a round-ribbed blaze-faced brown,
Shy as a country girl in town,
Scared of the gangway and scared of the quay,
Lathered in sweat at a sight of the sea,
But brave as a lion and strong as a bull,
With the mud at the hub in an uphill pull.
She learned her job as the best ones do,
And we hadn't been over a week or two
Before she would stand like a rooted oak
While the bullets whined and the shrapnel
    broke,
And a mile of the ridges rocked in glee,
As the shells went over from Battery B.

One by one our team went down,
But the gods were good to the blaze-faced
    brown
We swayed with the battles back and forth,
Lugging the limbers south and north.
Round us the world was red with flame
As we gained or gave in the changing game ;
Forward or backward, losses or gains,
There were empty saddles and idle chains,
For Death took some on the galloping track
And beckoned some from the bivouac ;
Till at last were left but my mare and me
Of all that went over with Battery B.

My mates have gone and left me alone ;
Their horses are heaps of ashes and bone.
Of all that went out in courage and speed
There is left but the little brown mare in the lead,
The little brown mare with the blaze on her face
That would die of shame at a slack in her trace,
That would swing the team to the least command,
That would charge a house at the slap of my hand,
That would turn from a shell to nuzzle my knee—
The pride and the wonder of Battery B.

I look for no praise and no ribbons to wear,
If I 've done my bit it was only my share,
For a man has his pride and the strength of his Cause
And the love of his home—they are unwritten laws.
But what of the horses that served at our side,
That in faith as of children fought with us and died ?

If I, through it all, have been true to my task,
I ask for no honours   This only I ask .
The gift of one gunner.
                              I know of a place
Where I 'd leave a brown mare with a blaze on her
        face,
'Mid low leafy lime-trees in cock's-foot and clover
To dream, with the dragon-flies glistening over.

THE TIMBER TEAM

(1918)

No medal and no cross they wear—
   No ribbon gleaming on the breast—
The burden that they bravely bear
   Only their daily tasks attest
Were Time to deal the just award
   Apportioned in God's wondrous scheme,
The Order of the Golden Sword
   Would blaze upon the Timber Team.

The axes called them to the woods,
   The humming round-saws sang them through ;
All down the scented solitudes
   Their chains made music as they drew.
With hearts that knew not how to flinch
   However sorely over-tried,
Across the torn moss inch by inch
   They hauled the butts along the ride.

And out upon the highway, churned
   And rutted by the ceaseless tyre,
Each day their matchless courage burned
   With new and never-ending fire.

EVERY 'COME ON, BILLY BOY!' STARTS A QUIVERING LIP;
WHAT CAN MAN DO MORE THAN GIVE 'EM WHIP AND STEEL!

('YOUNG ENGLAND.')

:

Beneath the chains their ribs were red,
  Their shoulders 'neath the collars scarred,
And yet with proud uplifted head
  Each night they reached the railway yard ,
Each grey of dawning sped them back
  Along the weary winding road,
With idle traces dangling slack,
  To lift another victory load.

Their gallant comrades overseas
  Have hauled the transport and the guns,
Yet scarcely known such stress as these—
  The patient unremembered ones.
If there are fields beyond the grave
  Where harried horses rest and dream,
Wide be the gateway for the Brave
  Whose toil was in the Timber Team !

A COMRADE

(1916)

You only know him groomed and combed
  And bridled on parade ;
I know the paddocks where he roamed,
  I saw him roped and made

I saw him on a Queensland plain
  Unbranded and unthrown,
With mud upon his tangled mane
  And forelock backward blown.

I saw him in the breaker's yard
  Bereft of half his pride,
The foam upon his shoulder starred,
  The sweat upon his side

He loved the wide-fenced fields, and I,
  Who loved those fields as dear,
Lived with him where the long plains lie
  Six hundred leagues from here.

You only know him groomed and combed,
  A charger on parade ;
I know the paddocks where he roamed
  Ere he was roped and made.

THE CLINK OF THE BIT

THE HORSEMAN

My song is of the Horseman—who woke the world's
    unrest,
To slake a king's ambition or serve a maid's behest ;
Who bore aloft the love-gage and reaped the rich
    reward ;
Who swayed the purple banner and swung the golden
    sword !

My song is of the Horseman ! steel wrist and iron
    thigh,
In whatsoever saddle, beneath whatever sky !
Who breaks the road for Empire , who leads the
    hope forlorn ;
Who rides with whip and knee-pad , who rides with
    rope and horn !

My song is of the Horseman who leads us through
    the vale,
Who dares the deepest river and risks the stoutest rail !
Who, 'neath the roaring race-stand, rides down to
    fence or fall ;
Who bends above the boar-spear ; who drives the
    dancing ball !

My song is of the Horseman, the centaurs of all time
Who stole for us the freedom of colts of every clime !
Who wore the spurs of mastery, who held the reins
    of pride,
Who left the world a heritage of sons to rule and ride !

Up ! Swear by bit and saddle-cloth, by crupper,
    cinch, and horn,
The spurs our grandsires buckled by our sons' sons
    shall be worn !
Let oil, nor steam, nor wings of dream deprive us
    of our own—
The wide world for a kingdom and the saddle for a
    throne !

GIPSIES' HORSES

MANY a time I 've wondered where the gipsies'
    horses go
When the caravans have faded from the lanes ;
When all the world of Romany lies buried in the
    snow,
    And not a rose of any fire remains.

Are there fairy-builded stables in the brown New
    Forest fern ?
Are there elfin stalls in Epping where they stand ?
Are they haltered in the heather by some haunted
    Highland burn,
    Where the blue hares change to witches out of
    hand ?

Are they feeding down the sunset in some opal land
    of dreams,
    Where the meadows stretch by rivers running gold ?
Is it there that we shall find them, all the piebalds
    and the creams,

Whatever roof may shelter them, whatever fields
    they tread,
  God grant them rest forgetful of the chains,
Till once again through England all the roses blossom
    red
  Of the gipsy fires alight along the lanes !

AN OLD CONTEMPTIBLE

ALONG the road the ceaseless motors thrust,
  Shrieking discordant warning and harsh blame.
Then, suddenly, proud stepping through the dust,
  Comes what I 'll call for want of better name
    One of the Old Contemptibles.

One of the good old sort , three-quarter bred ;
  Deep shouldered, long of rein, with ribs well-sprung
With honest eye and lean well-carried head ,
  With ears alert, now twitched, now forward flung.

Behind him rolls the high unhurried wheel ;
  His harness tinkles with a pleasing sound ;
With measured step his legs of hammered steel
  Lift merrily in music from the ground.

A fleck of foam upon his shoulder gleams,
  His nostrils quiver with the breath they drew ;
Over his forehead band his forelock streams,

What vision greets those patient blue-brown orbs ?
   What dim procession do the roads reveal ?
What fierce unfettered empery absorbs
   His once-sufficient realm of shaft and wheel ?

His not to question what the hours may bring ;
   His but to plod behind Time's swifter feet
Through that old world already on the wing
   The silence of the centuries to meet.

I find a sorrow in his stubborn stride ;
   With grief unguessed I stand and watch him go.
He carries with him much that nursed our pride ·
   Remembered things ;   things steadfast, staunch,
      and slow.

ADAM LINDSAY GORDON

(An equestrian statue of the poet is to be erected in
St Kilda Road, Melbourne)

' Two things stand like stone,' he said—
' Courage and Kindness ' Gallant Dead !
Long may the stone of his statue stand
That his fame may endure in his foster-land,
And never a careless world forget
That in this man Courage and Kindness met !

Many a rider in bronze and stone
Looks down on the street from his carven throne,
Clumsy and awkward and ill at ease
With a plunging charger between his knees ;
But—*Lindsay Gordon* ! By bar and bit
He shall sit in his saddle as horsemen sit !

Those that are slaves to the magic spell
Of the racing hoofs that he loved so well ;
Those that have tried to live straight and clean
' For the glory of God and for Gwendoline ! '
Shall greet him again as they pass below,

WHYTE-MELVILLE

WITH lightest of hands on the bridle, with lightest of
    hearts in the dance,
To the gods of Adventure and Laughter he quaffed
    the red wine of Romance,
Then wistfully turning the goblet he spilled the last
    drops at our feet,
And left us his tales to remember and left us his
    songs to repeat.

Where the trumpets of Babylon sounded we have
    ridden the sands at his side ,
Where Ishtar stood pale by the palm trees we have
    asked for no other as guide.
We have bowed to Valeria's beauty ; with Esca's
    our thoughts have gone home ;
We have shouted our ' Ave ! ' to Caesar with Hippias,
    swordsman of Rome.

By many a devious pathway, on many a far-away
    shore,
We have followed the brave Whyte-Melville in love
    and sport and war ;

We have ridden the wide world over, but always he
brought us back
To the red of the English woodlands and the cry of
an English pack.

If abroad in the asphodel meadows some Lord of the
Valley be found
That will try through the combes of the starlight the
courage of horse and of hound,
Could we ride to those infinite spaces girth deep
through the rose of the West,
We should find him once more on the Clipper dis-
puting the lead with the best.

And there with his peers we may leave him, with all
the good men and the true
Who have come to the Last of the Gateways and
laughed and gone galloping through ;
Where Kingsley for ever and ever to the chime of his
darlings may ride,
And Gordon, long-limbed upon Iseult, come stealing
the Cup by a stride !

BANSHEE

He stood there, chained to wall and rack
  With trebled steel. ' For God's own sake,'
The scared groom croaked to me, ' Stand back !
  You never know—*the chains might break !* '

Within the dim light of the stall
  I saw the wild eyes red with hate,
And marked the deep-set halter-gall
  That told the ceaseless strife with fate.

He heard a strange foot on the floor,
  A strange voice in the shadows sound,
And strained his fetters with a roar
  That shook the shed from roof to ground.

The foam upon his lips was white,
  His bitten breast was flecked with cream.
He screamed—a soul in piteous plight—
  Hate, fear, and anguish in the scream

' Why keep him tortured, chained and mad,
    And dungeoned from the daylight's gold ? '
' *His blood's the best we ever had,*
    And all his stock are sound and bold '

Maybe.—I crossed the sunlit lanes,
    And only saw, with eyes a-brim,
The torn brown breast, the trebled chains,
    The broken heart ; and wept for him.

A WINNING GOAL

WHAT though 'twas luck as much as skill that
    gathered up the pass,
Before us lies an open goal and eighty yards of grass.
Now, all ye gods of Hurlingham, come hearken to my
    call,
Give pace unto the twinkling feet that fly before
    them all !

Their Back is thwarted on the turn ; their Three 's
    out-thrown and wide ;
Their One and Two can scarce get through however
    hard they ride ;
So stretch your neck, my swift Babette, and lay
    you down at speed,
There 's not a flier on the field can rob you of the lead !

The dancing ball runs straight and true, the ground
    is fast as fire ,
To us remains the single stroke to crown our heart's
    desire.
With purple on their ponies' flanks they close on
    either side,
But you will keep in front, Babette, whose only spur
    is pride !

WITH PURPLE ON THEIR PONIES' FLANKS THEY CLOSE ON EITHER SIDE,
BUT YOU WILL KEEP IN FRONT, BABETTE, WHOSE ONLY SPUR IS PRIDE!

[A WINNING GOAL.]

One drive to make the trophy ours ! One glorious
    goal to get !—

The slow ball hangs and curves away. Swing in !
    Swing in, Babette !

Now ! How the tingle of the stroke through arm
    and shoulder spins !

A hefty hit . . . a deadly line . . . *a goal !* *The*
    goal that wins !

OUR GUESTS

(On the Menu Card of the Dinner given by *The Field*
to the American Polo Team, 25th June 1921)

WE welcome you,
Our guests from o'er the sea !
Together flew
Our flags till the world was free ;
And now they shall fly for us while we ride
In our rival friendship side by side.

With you we share
The love of the Greatest Game
Played clean and fair
For no reward but fame—
Fame and the Anglo-Saxon pride
In a goal to get and a horse to ride.

Win we or lose,
Clinch firm our vantage or fail,
Your galloping shoes
Our hearts are glad to hail ;
And here 's a health to the Big Twin Lands —
' Speed to our ponies ! Skill to our hands ! '

THE CIRCUS

Circus ! The gilded wagons ; the great tent
    blazing with light ,
The scent of the trampled sawdust and ' Three
    shilling seats to the right ' '
A face that peers through the curtain to see how the
    benches fill ;
The rustle of feet in the gangways ; the old expectant
    thrill.

Out of the lost years' twilight, clad in their spangles
    and gold,
Memory musters the riders that rode in the rings
    of old—
Knights and jockeys and jesters, piebald ponies and
    cream,
Fairies in satin and silver floating by in a dream.

Does the circle seem to us smaller that the cantering
    horses keep ?
Are they holding the big hoops lower where the

Ah ! well, there is one thing changeless—the gods be
    praised for that—
The peal of a small boy's laughter when the clown
    sits down on his hat.

CROOKÉD HOUSE TOLL

THE proud years have passed it and left it alone ;
  No more with red blossoms its gables are gay ,
From moss-covered thatch and from mouldering
    stone
  The rose that once wrapped it has withered
    away.
No longer the gate to a challenge is swung,
  Nor through it the old-fashioned chariots roll,
But I can remember the sixpennies flung,
  As we came at a canter through Crookéd House
    Toll.

A little old woman all wrinkled and brown,
  Like a russet-red pippin left long on the tree,
Would stand by the gate in her clean cotton gown
  And bob to our elders and smile upon me.
'Tis long since the lady relinquished her trust,
  But still I can picture on memory's scroll
The quaint little figure that stooped in the dust

When the moon's very round and the night's very
        still
    And the cottage is guest-room to goblin and gnome,
If you stand in the highway and look to the hill,
    You will see the brown horses come covered with
        foam,
You will hear the light tap of each hoof as it falls
    And the chink of the chains to the swing of the pole,
And see a white figure glide out from the walls
    To open the gate at the Crookéd House Toll.

THE STAR ON HIS FOREHEAD

The lift of his action is rhythmic and right,
His depth through the heart is a horseman's delight,
His tail flows to earth like the Falls of the Clyde,
The arch of his crest is the badge of his pride ;
There is flame in his nostril and fire in his eye ;
He is all that we look for, and boast of, and buy ;
All the marks of a good one are there to revere,
But the Star on his Forehead to me is most dear.

His make and his movement, his courage and fire
I accept and I value, I love and admire ;
The power of those quarters, those cannons of steel,
Those cool chiselled tendons clean run to the heel ;
All beauty !   All magic !

                        Yet one thing apart
From the pride of that picture stays close to my
      heart .
Not his strength, not his speed, not his line from
      Eclipse,
But the Star on his Forehead she touched with her

NEW FOREST PONIES

You are free of the woodland meadows,
  Of swamp and thicket and ride ;
All day in the slanting shadows
  You lurk and loiter and hide,
Till the moonlight silvers the bracken
  And the stars on the copses dance,
And the fires of the sunlight slacken
  As the night comes up from France !

The night that by tower and steeple
  Comes up like a witch in the sky,
Calling loud to the Little People
  To mount while the moon is high ;
Setting legions of light feet twinkling
  Through the dewy marshland grass,
And the bells on the heath-flower tinkling
  As the fairy horsemen pass !

In the light of the stars they gather
  Between the mirk and the morn,
With kirtle and cap and feather
  And hunting-knife and horn ;

Then come from the deep glades swinging
   Their ropes of the twisted dew,
Like gay little cowboys flinging
   Their lariat loops on you !

You are free of the woodland meadows,
   You are free of thicket and ride ,
All day in the slanting shadows
   You lurk and loiter and hide ;
All day unbitted and idle
   You wheel and whinny and prance,
But you bend to an elfin bridle
   When the night comes up from France !

AFTER THE THUNDER

If I 'd 'a had *two* I 'd 'a held 'em ; but just because
    I had four,
An' the black colt in for the first time, an' the bay
    mare lookin' for war,
Out of a bank o' purple came lightnin' splittin' the
    trees
An' playin' above the leaders an' drivin' 'em barmy
    as bees,
Wi' thunder crackin' across 'em as loud as the crack
    o' doom
Till I played for better-built harness an' a mile or
    two more o' room ,
For Dandy he lifted the bar-bit as light as a lady's
    thread,
An' Judy, she up wi' her wanton heels an' down wi'
    her damn little head ;
Then rip went his rotten-sewn traces—the colt was
    out over the bars ;
An' I said, as I looked at the lightnin', ' The next
    thing we 'll see 'll be stars ! '

But I braced my feet on the footboard and hammered
    the brake right back ;
I wasn't the man to be caught asleep, for I 've driven
    the Barwon track
For fifteen year wi' the Queensland mails, wi' four
    rough brutes to steer,
An' never a one you could hook to a bar without he
    was held by the ear !
So I took a pull an' a long cross-pull, an' I sawed
    'em good an' well,
For I 've had 'em bolt in the Queensland Bush wi'
    their mouths as tough as Hell ;
An', faith, but I had 'em back in hand when *crash*
    came another peal,
An' the colt let out a whistlin' snort an' the mare a
    vicious squeal,
An' a winker slewed an' a couplin' broke—an' away
    they went like mad,
An' I might ha' been dead in the stable loft for all
    the hope I had !

Now a Queensland team there 's a chance to stop,
    for they 're either too fat or thin ;
But these 'ere nags that the English drive, they are
    fit for a Derby win,
An' England herself is the size of a yard an' her
    roads is the width of a trough .

A gallop an' you 're at the island's edge, a kick an'
    you 're kicked right off !
' Now,' I says to myself, ' were you only out on the
    Thurulgoona plains
With a five-mile paddock to swing them in an' a
    bunch of Roma reins
You *might* have a chance ; but it looks, old son, as
    if your cake was dough
With a couplin' gone an' the winkers slipped an' a
    crowded road to go,
An' an island less than a saucer 's size to run your
    horses roun','
An' I says to myself, ' It 's no surprise if we finish
    it upside down ! '

    *   *   *   *   *   *

So that 's why I 'm here in an English ditch with the
    pole between my knees
An' people in motors bummin' about like a hive of
    hungry bees,
My leaders gone on the London Road a-draggin' my
    swingle-bars
Up an' down o' the Surrey hills an' in an' out o' the
    cars,
An' one o' my wheelers over the fence in a field of
    English wheat
An' the other lyin' dead on the road wi' my topper
    on one of his feet !—

An' the thunder 's gone, an' the sky is clear, an' the
    sun is shinin' bright,

An' *I* don't care—but my passengers, they got a Hell
    of a fright ;

An' if ever I drive that colt again when there 's
    thunder clouds about

I 'll hook 'im up wi' a bullock-chain an' a hook what
    won't come out !

AINTREE CALLS!

GALLOPS when the dawn is breaking,
Foam upon the breastplates flaking,
Upland turf to hoofbeats shaking,
    Lanterns in the dim-lit stalls.
Golden hopes that come to guide us,
Splendid dreams that float beside us ;
      Aintree calls !

Fences dark and water gleaming,
Colours down the straightway streaming,
    Glamour that the heart enthralls ;
Roar of crowds on crowds unending,
Hues upon the high stands blending,
Whistle of the whips descending ;
      Aintree calls !

Ghosts of men that here have ridden
Gather at the post unbidden,
    Waiting till the old flag falls ;
Hear the rattled guard-rails quiver
As they rush them, game as ever !
(Mist, O mist, on Mersey River !)
      Aintree calls !

Danger beckons yet to daring,
And the colours wait for wearing,
While Fame proffers gifts for sharing
    And Dame Fortune plans the falls.
Lo ! the spirit of endeavour
Burns in England's heart for ever ;
    Aintree calls !

THE STALLION

BESIDE the dusty road he steps at ease ;
   His great head bending to the stallion-bar,
Now lifted, now flung downward to his knees,
   Tossing the forelock from his forehead star ;
Champing the while his heavy bit in pride
And flecking foam upon his flank and side.

Save for his roller striped in white and blue
   He bears no harness on his mighty back ;
For all the splendour of his bone and thew
   He travels burdenless along the track,
Yet shall he give a hundred hefty sons
The strength to carry what his kingship shuns

The pheasants rustling on the roadside bank,
   The pigeons swinging out in sudden chase,
Break not his broad shoes' rhythmic clank
   Nor set him swerving from his measured pace.
He knows the road and all its hidden fears,
His the staid calm that comes with conquering years

WHEN YOUR HOMING CARLOADS SWING
PAST US DOWN THE CRISPING LANES.

(*HACKING HOME.*)

He snatches at the clover as he goes,
  Clinking the bit-chain as he gathers toll ;
He sniffs the speedwell, through wide nostrils blows,
  And but for chain and bar would kneel and roll
His eyes alone reveal in smouldering fire
Pride held in leash, reined Lust and curbed Desire.

TO HORSE AND AWAY

When sorrows come sobbing
    To clutch at the breast,
When trouble comes robbing
    The heart of its rest,
When cash columns addle
    The brain as they may ;
Swing into the saddle,
    To horse and away !
    To horse and away
    To the heart of the fray !
Fling Care to the Devil for one merry day !

When tradesmen importune,
    When duns make advance,
When fickle Dame Fortune
    Is frowning askance,
When Love 's looking lonely
    And Life 's looking grey,
There 's one solace only—
    To horse and away !
    To horse and away
    With spurs in the bay !
Sling Care to perdition for one merry day !

Behind each gay rider
  Sits Care, we are told,
With dark hair to hide her,
  And clinging hands cold ;
If swift we be flying
  Care cannot but sway
And fall ! Leave her lying ;
  To horse and away !
  To horse and away !
  Where she fell let her stay !
Hark for'ard ! And leave her—Care dead for a day !

THE GOLDEN HOOFPRINTS

I WALKED one day on a road in Devon—
   A road that rose till it touched the blue,
Where high in the curtained halls of Heaven
   The God of all beauty reigned, I knew.

Out of the dawn had a light snow drifted,
   The line of the road was limned in white,
And over the edge of the world it lifted
   Beautiful, burnished, broad and bright.

A horseman had passed in the morning early,
   Each hoof of his steed had left its mould,
And now as the noon sun caught them fairly
   Every track was a curve of gold.

The snow was a highway white to Heaven,
   Golden-flecked where the hoofprints lay ;
And there 's many a fairy lane in Devon,
   But this was surely the Wonder-Way !

WIND OF THE NIGHT

HARK to the high wind's hunting horn !
The hounds of the night run mute and fast,
You may hear a branch from the beech-tree torn
As the Field goes trampling past ;
Where the moonlit miles lie silver white,
Luck to your hunting, wind of the night !

Wide is the rippling river spread
(Up and over and on and away ')
Somewhere the pack is running ahead
Into the woodland strips of Day
For'ard on to the morning light !
Luck to your hunting, wind of the night !

What are they running ?   The scented drag
Of the shy dark's rustling feet ?
The rosy trail of the sunset stag,
Or the dawn fox grey and fleet ?—
Blow them on, for they 're running right !
Luck to your hunting, wind of the night !

THE HOOFS OF THE HORSES

The hoofs of the horses !—Oh ! witching and sweet
Is the music earth steals from the iron-shod feet ;
No whisper of love1, no trilling of bird
Can stir me as hoofs of the horses have stirred.

They spurn disappointment and trample despair,
And drown with their drum-beats the challenge of
      care ;
With scarlet and silk for their banners above,
They are swifter than Fortune and sweeter than Love.

On the wings of the morning they gather and fly,
In the hush of the night-time I hear them go by—
The horses of memory thundering through
With flashing white fetlocks all wet with the dew.

When you lay me to slumber no spot you can choose
But will ring to the rhythm of galloping shoes,
And under the daisies no grave be so deep
But the hoofs of the horses shall sound in my sleep.

Milton Keynes UK
Ingram Content Group UK Ltd.
UKHW022029111223
434204UK00005B/147